Harmonica cards
new variations

Annelies Karduks

FORTE PUBLISHERS

Contents

© 2004 Forte Uitgevers, Utrecht
© 2004 for the translation by the publisher
Original title: *Harmonicakaarten nieuwe variaties*

All rights reserved.
No part of this publication may be copied, stored in an electronic file or made public, in any form or in any way whatsoever, either electronically, mechanically, by photocopying or any other form of recording, without the publisher's prior written permission.

ISBN 90 5877 449 X

This is a publication from
Forte Publishers BV
P.O. Box 1394
3500 BJ Utrecht
The Netherlands

For more information about the creative books available from
Forte Uitgevers:
www.forteuitgevers.nl

Final editing: Gina Kors-Lambers, Steenwijk, the Netherlands
Photography and digital image editing: Fotografie Gerhard Witteveen, Apeldoorn, the Netherlands
Cover and inner design:
BADE creatieve communicatie, Baarn, the Netherlands
Translation: Michael Ford, TextCase, Hilversum, the Netherlands

Preface	3
Techniques	4
Step-by-step	5
Materials	7
Card on the cover	7
Flowers	8
Mini harmonica cards	10
Small flowers	14
Roses and Lathyrus	18
Photographs	22
More flowers	24
Christmas decorations	27
Flat Christmas cards	31

Preface

After the wonderful reaction to the first book, **Harmonica folding**, and the templates, it did not take long for a second book to be published. I have, of course, designed new templates and new rulers for this book. The templates from the first and second books can all be used together. The old templates can be used with the new rulers and the new templates can be used with the old rulers, so that there are many more possibilities which are not shown in this book.

I think it is great that my daughters also come up with new designs for cards. Robine thought up the mini harmonica cards and Larissa designed one of the cards made using ruler F. I really like the fact that they are so supportive.

See page 32 if you wish to remain informed of what I have in store for you in the future.

I wish you lots of fun with these harmonica cards.

Techniques

Carefully read these instructions and look at the Step-by-step photographs before starting.

Guide lines for the templates

- The templates are 14.85 cm high and you can use them to cut the cards to the correct size.
- There is a black line on the templates to indicate the middle.
- The templates have two black lines which are 10.5 cm apart. If you make a card which is 10.5 cm high, then you must keep the bottom black line level with the bottom of the card and the top black line level with the top of the card.
- The new templates have two arrows on them which are 6 cm apart. When making a mini harmonica card, which is 6 cm high, keep the bottom arrow level with the bottom of the card and the top arrow level with the top of the card.

Using the harmonica rulers

Choose the card you wish to make. Read the instructions and cut the card to the correct size. The instructions also tell you which harmonica ruler to use. The harmonica rulers are drawn on the packaging of the templates. Use the ruler to draw lines at the top and bottom of the card. The harmonica ruler indicates which lines are used to cut shapes and which lines are used to score uninterrupted score lines. Score the uninterrupted lines first to avoid making any mistakes (see photograph 1). If necessary, draw the lines to mark the height of the card.

Cutting harmonica cards

When cutting harmonica cards, look on the ruler for the "‹-" sign, the "-›" sign or the "^-" sign. The "‹-" sign indicates that the cut shape points to the left, the "›-" sign indicates that the cut shape points to the right and the "^-" sign indicates that the cut shape points upwards. Use template tape to stick the harmonica template level with the lines on the left-hand side. Cut the shape(s) and score the straight sides along the template for cards E and F (see photograph 2). Repeat this for the next lines with a "‹-" sign, a "-›" sign or a "^-" sign. It is important to not cut through the uninterrupted score lines. To avoid doing so, use the smaller cutting shape (see photograph 3). Cut the middle pieces of card H to the correct height and cut the end off.

Card F: Draw lines using the harmonica ruler and score the uninterrupted score lines. Cut the card to the correct height. Draw the lines that have been cut off on the card again.

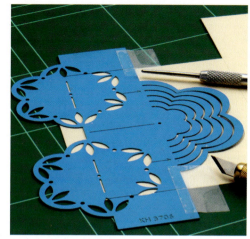

Stick the harmonica template down, level with the lines farthest to the left and cut out the shape.

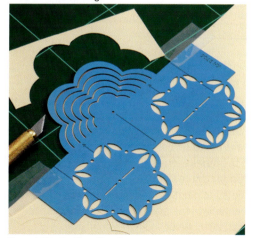

Repeat this for the other lines.

Fold the card. Rub the lines out.

STEP-BY-STEP

Folding the card

Fold the uninterrupted score lines first and then the score lines interrupted by shapes. On the ruler, you will see whether you must make a valley fold or a mountain fold (see photograph 4).

All the harmonica cards fit in a standard envelope if they are folded double along the score lines.

Decorating the card

Embossing
Cut the shapes out as explained in the instructions. Stick the template to a light box. Use template tape to stick the card on the template with the good side facing downwards and copy the illuminated shapes using the embossing stylus. If you wish, you can use Pergasoft to make the embossing easier.

Stamp-pad ink
Stamp-pad ink gives the best results when you emboss first. After embossing, turn the template and the shape over and place them on your work surface. Dip a stamp sponge on the ink pad and sponge the pattern on the shape. Allow the ink to dry.

Cutting
Hold a sharp knife vertically and cut the lines in the template. Remove the template and cut through every other middle piece.

Cutting half-shapes
Place the template level with the edge of the card so that only the shape is on the card and then cut out the half-shape.

Cutting out separate decorations
Place the template level with the edge of the card so that only the shape is on the card and then cut out the decorations, starting with the smallest cutting line.

Punch decorations
Use punch paper (120 gram). Stand up when punching. Place the punch on a hard surface with the knob facing downwards. Slide the shape into the punch, making sure that, if there is a pattern, it is facing upwards. Once the shape is in the punch properly, press the punch down slightly with one hand so that the shape gets firmly stuck in the punch. Put two thumbs and a bent forefinger around the punch opening and press the punch down. Remove all the small pieces of paper. Repeat this as often as necessary.

Materials

- Card and paper:
  cArt-us (CA), Mi-teintes
  Canson (C) and Papicolor (P)
- Harmonica templates
- Scoring pen
- Cutting ruler with a metal edge
- Cutting mat
- Hobby knife
- Template tape
- 3D cutting sheets
- Tweezer scissors
- Photo glue
- 3D foam tape/blocks and/or silicon glue
- Light box
- Embossing stylus
- Eyelet tool
- Hammer
- Pencil
- Rubber
- Pritt non-permanent glue roller

Card on the cover

What you need:
- Card: natural CA211 (P03) and apple green C475
- 3 cutting sheets: MD tulipa (no. 420)
- Mine eyelet rings (red)
- Charms EE4304
- Gold thread

Cut the natural card to size (14.85 x 29.7 cm). Use harmonica ruler F and the outer edge of the template to cut the card. Cut, score and fold the harmonica card. Use the extra cutting lines in the template to cut the decorations. Cut two green strips (3.5 x 10.5 cm) and stick them on the card. Make the pictures 3D.

Flowers

See Techniques for instructions on how to decorate the cards.

What you need:
- ❏ Card: natural CA211 (P03) and apple green C475

Card 1
Extra materials:
- ❏ Charms EE4301
- ❏ Round Bradletz (gold)
- ❏ 3 cutting sheets: MD rosa (no. 413)
- ❏ Scribbles glittering crystal

Cut the card to size (14.85 x 29.7 cm). Use harmonica ruler F and the largest cutting line in the template to cut the card. Cut, score and fold the harmonica card. Use the extra cutting lines in the harmonica template to cut the decorations. Cut two green strips (3.5 x 10.5 cm) and stick them on the card. Cut out a green square (8 x 8 cm). Use a Bradletz to attach the Charm. Make the pictures 3D. Add Scribbles to the rose.

Card 2
Extra materials:
- ❏ 3 cutting sheets: MD tulipa (no. 420)

Cut the card to size (10.5 x 29.7 cm). Use harmonica ruler F and the largest cutting line in the template to cut the card. Cut, score and fold the harmonica card. Use the extra cutting lines in the template to cut the decorations. Use the template to cut the green decorations and stick them on the card. Cut out a green rectangle (7.5 x 10.5 cm). Make the pictures 3D.

Card 3
Extra materials:
- ❏ 3 cutting sheets: MD viola (no. 417)

Cut the card to size (10.5 x 29.7 cm). Use harmonica ruler F and the outer edge of the template to cut the card. Cut, score and fold the harmonica card. Use the extra cutting lines in the template to cut the decorations. Use the template to cut the green decorations and stick them on the card. Cut out a green rectangle (7.5 x 10.5 cm). Make the pictures 3D.

Card 4
Extra materials:
- ❏ Mini adhesive stones (red)
- ❏ 3 cutting sheets: MD daisy (no. 415)

Cut the card to size (14.85 x 29.7 cm). Use harmonica ruler F and the outer edge of the template to cut the card. Cut, score and fold the harmonica card. Use the extra cutting lines in the harmonica template to cut the decorations. Cut two green strips (3.5 x 10.5 cm) and stick them on the card. Cut out a green rectangle (7.5 x 10 cm). Stick the adhesive stones on the card. Make the pictures 3D.

FLOWERS 9

Mini harmonica cards

See Techniques for instructions on how to decorate the cards. The new templates have two arrows on them which are 6 cm apart. When making mini harmonica cards, keep the bottom arrow level with the bottom of the card and the top arrow level with the top of the card. For the first set of templates, the largest cutting line in the template has a 6 cm gap.

Card 1

What you need:
- Card: light blue CA391 (P42) and cornflower blue CA393
- Silver line stickers
- Mini eyelets (silver)
- Funny Fibre (assorted blue)
- Cutting sheet: Quadrant (IT 403)
- Scribbles glittering crystal

Cut the card to size (6 x 21 cm). Use the second cutting line from the middle of harmonica ruler G. Cut, score and fold the harmonica card. Stick three sets of two line stickers on the card. Use the template to cut three half-flowers. Copy pattern A onto printing paper and cut out the pattern. Use the Pritt roller to stick the pattern on the card and punch the eyelet holes. Thread a Funny Fibre through the eyelets. Make the flowers 3D. Add Scribbles to the flowers.

Card 2

What you need:
- Card: natural CA211 (P03) and apple green C475
- Mini eyelets (silver)
- Funny Fibre (assorted orange)
- Cutting sheet: MD daisy (no. 415)
- Small 6-leaf flower punch
- Silver sticker dots

Cut the card to size (6 x 21 cm). Use the third cutting line from the middle of harmonica ruler G. Cut, score and fold the harmonica card. Cut out three green squares (3.3 x 3.3 cm). Copy pattern A onto printing paper and cut out the pattern. Use the Pritt roller to stick the pattern on the card and punch the eyelet holes. Thread a Funny Fibre through the eyelets. Make the flowers 3D. Punch the flowers and stick a sticker dot in the middle.

Card 3

What you need:
- Card: light blue CA391 (P42) and cornflower blue CA393
- Silver line stickers
- Mini eyelets (silver)
- Basic figure eyelet tags
- Cutting sheet: Quadrant (IT 404)
- Silver text sticker
- Permanent dark blue marker pen

Cut the card to size (6 x 21 cm). Use the third cutting line from the middle of harmonica ruler G. Cut, score and fold the harmonica card. Stick three line stickers on the card. Use the template to cut three semicircles. Use an eyelet to attach the tag to the card. Decorate the tag with a blue text sticker. Make the flowers 3D.

Card 4

What you need:
- ❏ Card: natural CA211 (P03) and apple green C475
- ❏ Metallic fun eyelet shapes (silver)
- ❏ Mini eyelet rings (silver)
- ❏ Funny Fibre (assorted yellow)
- ❏ Cutting sheet: MD viola (no. 417)
- ❏ Silver text sticker
- ❏ Punch: small and medium-sized 6-leaf flower

Cut the card to size (6 x 21 cm). Use the second cutting line from the middle of harmonica ruler G. Cut, score and fold the harmonica card. Copy pattern B three times onto printing paper and cut the shapes out slightly bigger. Use the Pritt roller to stick the shapes on green card and cut the labels out carefully. Use an eyelet to attach them to the card. Punch the flowers and use an eyelet to attach a large flower in the corner of the card. Thread a Funny Fibre through the eyelet. Make the flowers 3D.

Card 5

What you need:
- ❏ Card: fiesta red P12 (CA517) and white CA210 (P30)
- ❏ Cutting sheets: Mini Christmas decorations IT 387 and mini candles IT 388

Cut the card to size (6 x 21 cm). Use the second cutting line from the middle of harmonica ruler G. Cut, score and fold the harmonica card. Use the template to cut three half-stars. Stick part of the border decorations from the cutting sheet on the card. Make the Christmas decorations 3D.

Card 6

What you need:
- ❏ Card: golden yellow CA247 (P10) and apple green C475
- ❏ Metallic fun eyelet shapes (green)
- ❏ Funny Fibre (assorted green)
- ❏ Cutting sheet: Marjoleine daisies

Cut the card to size (6 x 21 cm). Use the third cutting line from the middle of harmonica ruler G. Cut, score and fold the harmonica card. Cut out three green squares (3.5 x 3.5 cm). Copy pattern A onto printing paper and cut out the pattern. Use the Pritt roller to stick the pattern on the card and punch the eyelet holes. Thread a Funny Fibre through the eyelets. Make the daisies 3D. Make the butterflies 3D.

Card 7

What you need:
- Card: fiesta red P12 (CA517) and white CA210 (P30)
- Cutting sheet: mini Christmas decorations IT 387
- Silver star stickers

Cut the card to size (6 x 21 cm). Use the second cutting line from the middle of harmonica ruler G. Cut, score and fold the harmonica card. Use the template to cut three half-triangles. Stick part of the border decorations from the cutting sheet on the card as well as the star stickers. Make the Christmas decorations 3D.

Card 8

What you need:
- Card: golden yellow CA247 (P10) and apple green C475
- Metallic fun eyelet shapes (green)
- Dark green raffia
- Cutting sheet: Marjoleine violets

Cut the card to size (6 x 21 cm). Use the third cutting line from the middle of harmonica ruler G. Cut, score and fold the harmonica card. Use the template to cut three half-octagons. Copy pattern A onto printing paper and cut out the pattern. Use the Pritt roller to stick the pattern on the card and punch the eyelet holes. Thread raffia through the eyelets. Make the violets 3D.

Pattern A

Pattern B

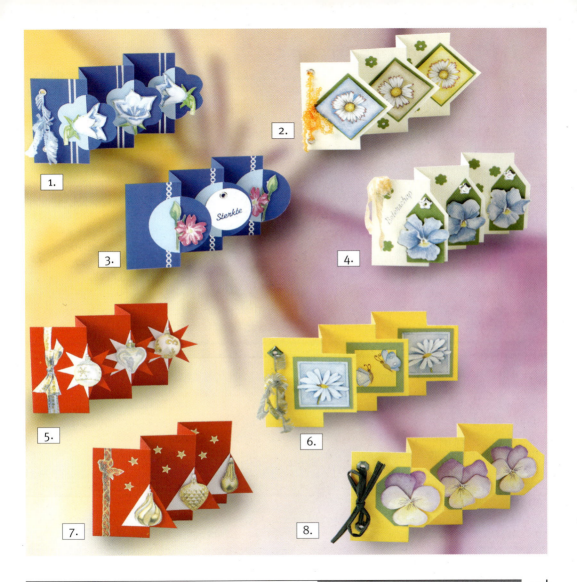

MINI HARMONICA CARDS 13

Small flowers

What you need
- ❏ Card: light blue CA391 (P42) and aqua marine CA427
- ❏ Paper: light blue CA391 (P42) and aqua marine CA427
- ❏ Ruler C in pieces (see patterns C1, C2 and C3)
- ❏ Double-sided adhesive tape

Card 1

Extra materials:
- ❏ Round Bradletz (gold)
- ❏ Ornament corner punch: Fantasy 2
- ❏ Cutting sheet: Quadrant (IT 403)

Cut a piece of card to 10 x 14.85 cm for part C1, to 11 x 14.85 cm for part C2 and to 10.7 x 14.85 cm for part C3. Use patterns C1, C2 and C3. Use the top shape for C1, the middle shape with the arrows for part C2 and the bottom shape for part 3. Cut, score and fold the harmonica card and use double-sided adhesive tape to stick the pieces together. Copy pattern D twice onto light blue paper and once onto aqua marine paper and punch the strips. Cut two 3 cm wide aqua marine strips and one 3 cm wide light blue strip. Stick all the strips on the card. Copy pattern H three times onto light blue paper and cut out the smallest labels. Punch the labels and use a Bradletz to attach them to the card. Make the flowers 3D.

Card 2

Extra materials:
- ❏ Ornament corner punch: Fantasy 4
- ❏ Cutting sheet: Quadrant (IT 401)

Cut a piece of card to 10 x 14.85 cm for part C1, to 11 x 14.85 cm for part C2 and to 9.5 x 14.85 cm for part C3. Use patterns C1, C2 and C3. Use the top shape for C1, the middle shape with the arrows for part C2 and the bottom shape for part 3. Cut, score and fold the harmonica card and use double-sided adhesive tape to stick the pieces together. Copy pattern E twice onto light blue paper and once onto aqua marine paper. Punch the strips. Cut two 3 cm wide aqua marine strips and one 3 cm wide light blue strip. Stick all the strips on the card. Make the flowers 3D.

Card 3

Extra materials:
- ❏ Corner ornament punch: flower and dots
- ❏ Cutting sheet: Quadrant (IT 402)
- ❏ Mini adhesive stones (white)

Cut a piece of card to 10 x 14.85 cm for part C1, to 11 x 14.85 cm for part C2 and to 10.7 x 14.85 cm for part C3. Use patterns C1, C2 and C3.

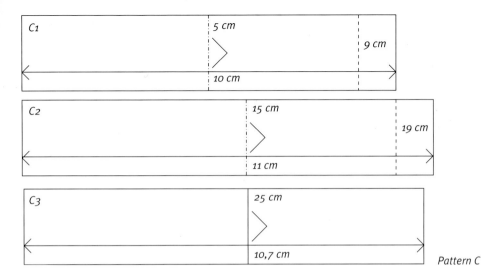

Pattern C

Use the top shape for C1, the middle shape with the arrows for part C2 and the bottom shape for part 3. Cut, score and fold the harmonica card and use double-sided adhesive tape to stick the pieces together. Copy pattern F three times onto light blue paper and punch the strips. Cut a 2.5 cm wide aqua marine strip. Stick all the strips on the card. Make the flowers 3D. Decorate the card with adhesive stones.

Card 4
Extra materials:
- ❏ Ornament corner punch: Fantasy 3
- ❏ Cutting sheet: Quadrant (IT 404)
- ❏ Mini adhesive stones (white)

Cut a piece of card to 10 x 14.85 cm for part C1, to 11 x 14.85 cm for part C2 and to 10.7 x 14.85 cm for part C3. Use patterns C1, C2 and C3. Use the top shape for C1, the largest cutting line in the template of the middle shape for part C2 and the bottom shape for part 3. Cut, score and fold the harmonica card and use double-sided adhesive tape to stick the pieces together. Copy pattern G twice onto light blue paper and once onto aqua marine paper and punch the strips. Make four light blue rectangles and one aqua marine rectangle (2.5 x 5 cm). Stick everything on the card. Make the flowers 3D.

Pattern D (125%)

Pattern E (125%)

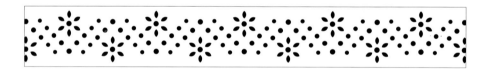

Pattern F (125%)

Pattern G (125%)

SMALL FLOWERS

Roses and Lathyrus

What you need:
- ❏ Card: white CA210 (P30)

Card 1

Extra materials:
- ❏ Sharon Ann scrapbook paper (red garden)
- ❏ Stamp-pad ink: scarlet and ruby
- ❏ Stamp sponges
- ❏ Fiskars border ornament punch (lace)
- ❏ Cutting sheet: yellow roses IT 399
- ❏ Charms EE4301
- ❏ Round Bradletz (gold)
- ❏ Gold text sticker

Cut the card to size (14.85 x 21 cm) using harmonica ruler E. Note: cut the shapes in the opposite direction as indicated on the ruler. Use the outer edge of the template. Cut, score and fold the harmonica card. Cut a 10.5 cm wide strip of green printed scrapbook paper and a 7 cm wide strip of red scrapbook paper. Punch both sides of the strips. Fold the punched strips in two and stick one side on the card. Allow them to dry and then stick the other side on the card. Fold the card closed so that the paper sits in the fold nicely. Dab the sides of the card and the shapes with stamp-pad ink. Use a Bradletz to attach the Charm. Make the pictures 3D.

Card 2

Extra materials:
- ❏ Sharon Ann scrapbook paper (red garden)
- ❏ Stamp-pad ink: scarlet and ruby
- ❏ Stamp sponges
- ❏ Fiskars border ornament punch (Sunflower)
- ❏ Cutting sheet: pink roses IT 400

Cut the card to size (14.85 x 21 cm) using harmonica ruler E. Note: cut the shapes in the opposite direction as indicated on the ruler. Use the outer edge of the template. Cut, score and fold the harmonica card. Cut a 4 cm wide strip of green printed scrapbook paper and an 11 cm wide strip of red scrapbook paper. Punch both sides of the strips. Fold the red, punched strip in two and stick one side on the card. Allow it to dry and then stick the other side on the card. Fold the card closed so that the paper sits in the fold nicely. Cut the green, punched strip in two and stick the two halves on the sides of the card. Dab the sides of the shapes with stamp-pad ink. Make the pictures 3D.

Card 3

Extra materials:
- ❏ Sharon Ann scrapbook paper (green garden)
- ❏ Decoration chalks
- ❏ 3 cutting sheets: white Lathyrus IT 395

❏ *Metallic fun eyelet shapes (purple)*
❏ *Gold text sticker*

Cut the card to size (14.85 x 21 cm) using harmonica ruler E. Use the outer edge of the template. Cut, score and fold the harmonica card. Tear green and white printed scrapbook paper and stick it on the card. Fold the white strip for the middle of the card in two and stick one side on the card. Allow it to dry and then stick the other side on the card. Fold the card closed so that the paper sits in the fold nicely. Copy pattern H onto printing paper and cut the shape out slightly bigger.

Use the Pritt roller to stick the shape on white card and cut the label out carefully. Dab the sides of the shapes and the label with purple chalk. Use an eyelet to attach the label to the card. Make the pictures 3D.

Card 4

Extra materials:
❏ *Sharon Ann scrapbook paper (green garden)*
❏ *Decoration chalks*
❏ *3 cutting sheets: pink Lathyrus IT 396*

Cut the card to size (14.85 x 21 cm) using harmonica ruler E. Use the outer edge of the template. Cut, score and fold the harmonica card. Cut two 5 cm wide strips from green printed scrapbook paper. Punch both sides of the strips. Stick the strips and the punched flowers on the card. Cut out two small green squares (4.5 x 4.5 cm) and two white squares (4 x 4 cm). Stick the white squares on the green square and use foam tape to stick this on the card. Make the pictures 3D.

Pattern H

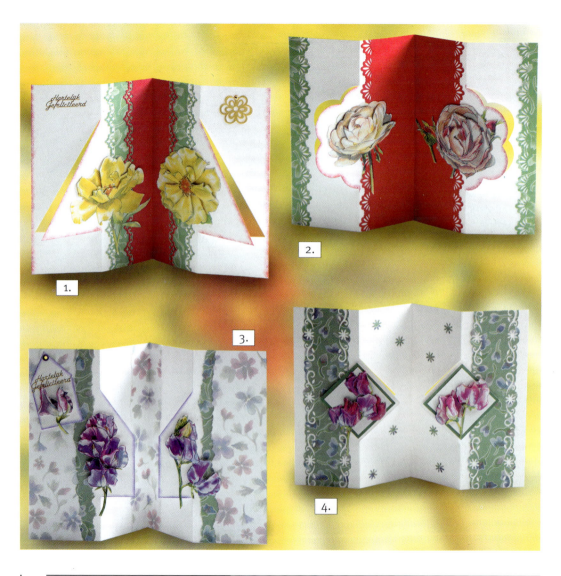

20 ROSES AND LATHYRUS

Photographs

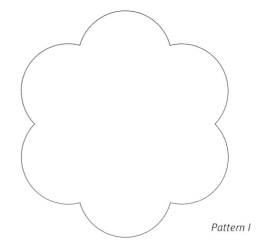

Pattern I

What you need:
- ❏ Card: dark blue CA417 (P41), red CA517 (P12) and white C335 (P03)
- ❏ Paper: dark blue CA417 (P41) and red CA517 (P12)

Card 1

Extra materials:
- ❏ Stamp-pad ink: scarlet and royal blue
- ❏ Stamp sponges
- ❏ Modern monogram alphabet
- ❏ Strips of red tissue paper

Cut the card to size (14.85 x 29.7 cm) using harmonica ruler F. Cut, score and fold the harmonica card. Stick the photograph (7.5 x 14.85 cm) in the middle of the card. Stick strips of red tissue paper on the card. Copy pattern I four times onto printing paper and cut the shapes out slightly bigger. Use the Pritt roller to stick the shapes on white card and use the template to cut the flowers out along the lines. Emboss the flowers and the letters and decorate everything with stamp-pad ink. Stick the shapes on the card.

Card 2

Extra materials:
- ❏ Embellishments: silver/white ice-crystal
- ❏ Stamp-pad ink: royal blue
- ❏ Stamp sponge
- ❏ Jumbo snowflake punch

Cut the card to size (14.85 x 29.7 cm) using harmonica ruler F. Cut, score and fold the harmonica card. Cut out a red rectangle (9.8 x 14.85 cm). Stick the photograph (8.8 x 13.8 cm) in the middle of the card. Copy pattern J four times onto printing paper and cut the shapes out slightly bigger. Use the Pritt roller to stick the shapes on white card and cut the largest stars out along the outer lines. Emboss the stars and decorate the patterns with stamp-pad ink. Punch four blue snowflakes. Stick everything on the card.

Card 3

Extra materials:
- ❏ Stamp-pad ink: royal blue
- ❏ Stamp sponge

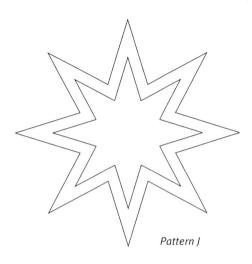

Pattern J

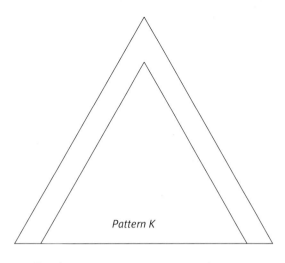

Pattern K

- ❏ Punches: lily and jumbo lily
- ❏ Metallic fun eyelet shapes (dark blue)

Cut the card to size (14.85 x 29.7 cm) using harmonica ruler F. Cut, score and fold the harmonica card. Cut two 2.5 cm wide white strips and two 2 cm wide red strips. Cut out a red rectangle (9.8 x 14.85 cm). Stick the strips and the rectangle on the card. Stick the photograph (8.8 x 13.8 cm) in the middle of the card. Copy pattern H four times onto printing paper and cut the shapes out slightly bigger. Use the Pritt roller to stick the shapes on white card and cut the largest labels out along the outer lines. Use the template to position the eyelet. Emboss the labels and use stamp-pad ink to decorate the patterns. Use eyelets to attach the labels to the card. Punch the lilies and stick them on the card using foam tape.

Card 4

Extra materials:
- ❏ Stamp-pad ink: royal blue
- ❏ Stamp sponge
- ❏ Punches: small, medium-sized and large 6-leaf flower

Cut the card to size (14.85 x 29.7 cm) using harmonica ruler F. Rotate the template until it is in the desired position and then cut, score and fold the harmonica card. Cut out a red rectangle (9.8 x 14.85 cm). Stick the photograph (8.8 x 13.8 cm) in the middle of the card. Copy pattern K four times onto printing paper and cut the shapes out slightly bigger. Use the Pritt roller to stick the shapes on white card and cut the triangles out along the lines. Emboss the triangles and use stamp-pad ink to decorate the patterns. Punch the flowers and stick them on the card using foam tape.

More flowers

What you need:
- Card: apple green C475
- Gold line stickers

Card 1

Extra materials:
- Card: golden yellow CA247 (P10)
- Metallic fun eyelet shapes (purple)
- 3 cutting sheets: Marjoleine violets

Cut the card to size (14.85 x 29.7 cm) using harmonica ruler H. Use the cutting line with the arrows or the outer edge of the template with the two shapes on one side. Cut, score and fold the harmonica card. Use the extra cutting lines in the harmonica template to cut the decorations. Use a pencil to mark the position of the eyelets, punch the eyelet holes and attach the eyelets. Cut out one large green square (6 x 6 cm) and two small green squares (4 x 4 cm). Decorate the squares with line stickers. Make the violets 3D.

Card 2

Extra materials:
- Card: golden yellow CA247 (P10)
- Metallic fun eyelet shapes (dark blue)
- 2 cutting sheets: Marjoleine daisies

Cut the card to size (14.85 x 29.7 cm) using harmonica ruler H. Use the cutting line with the arrows or the outer edge of the template with the two shapes on one side. Cut, score and fold the harmonica card. Use the extra cutting lines in the harmonica template to cut the decorations. Use a pencil to mark the positions of the eyelets, punch the eyelet holes and attach the eyelets. Cut out one large green square (7 x 7 cm) and two small green squares (5 x 5 cm). Decorate the squares with line stickers. Make the daisies 3D.

Card 3

Extra materials:
- Card: pink CA481 (P34)
- 3 cutting sheets: Marjoleine pink roses
- Gold text sticker

Cut the card to size (14.85 x 29.7 cm) using harmonica ruler H. Use the outer edge of the template with the two shapes on one side. Cut, score and fold the harmonica card. Cut out one large green square (7 x 7 cm) and two small green squares (4 x 4 cm). Decorate the squares with line stickers. Make the roses 3D.

Card 4

Extra materials:
- Card: pink CA481 (P34)
- Metallic fun eyelet shapes (pink)
- 2 cutting sheets: Marjoleine pink tulips
- Gold text sticker

Cut the card to size (14.85 x 29.7 cm) using harmonica ruler H. Use the cutting line with the arrows or the outer edge of the template with the two shapes on one side. Cut, score and fold the harmonica card. Cut out one large green square (7 x 7 cm) and two small green squares (4 x 4 cm). Decorate the squares with line stickers. Copy pattern B three times onto printing paper and cut the shapes out slightly bigger. Use the Pritt roller to stick the shapes on green card and cut the labels out along the lines. Use eyelets to attach the labels to the card and decorate them with a text sticker. Make the tulips 3D.

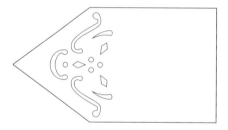

Pattern L

Pattern M

MORE FLOWERS

Christmas decorations

What you need:
- ❏ Card: fiesta red P12 (CA517) and golden yellow P141
- ❏ Paper: fiesta red P12 (CA517) and golden yellow P141
- ❏ Cutting sheets: mini Christmas decorations IT 387 and mini candles IT 388

Card 1

Extra materials:
- ❏ Round Bradletz (gold)
- ❏ Fiskars border ornament punch (Holly)
- ❏ Ornament corner punch: Fantasy 3

Cut the card to size (14.85 x 21 cm) using harmonica ruler E. Cut, score and fold the harmonica card. Cut two 3.5 cm wide red strips and one 4 cm wide red strip. Punch the 3.5 cm strips on one side and the 4 cm strip on both sides. Fold the strip for the middle of the card in two and stick one side on the card. Allow it to dry and then stick the other side on the card. Fold the card closed so that the paper sits in the fold nicely. Stick the other strips and some of the border decorations from the cutting sheet on the card. Copy pattern L three times onto red paper and cut out the labels. Punch the labels and use a Bradletz to attach them to the card. Stick the Christmas decorations on the card using foam tape.

Card 2

Extra materials:
- ❏ Round Bradletz (gold)
- ❏ Mosaic ornament punch: star/lily
- ❏ Charms EE4303

Cut the card to size (14.85 x 21 cm) using harmonica ruler E. Cut, score and fold the harmonica card. Cut two 3 cm wide gold strips.

28 CHRISTMAS DECORATIONS

FLAT CHRISTMAS CARDS 29

Copy pattern M twice onto red paper and punch the strips. Copy pattern J three times onto gold paper and cut out the smallest stars. Stick everything on the card. Use a Bradletz to attach the Charm. Stick the Christmas decorations on the card using foam tape.

Card 3

Extra materials:
❏ Round Bradletz (gold)

Cut the card to size (14.85 x 21 cm) using harmonica ruler E. Cut, score and fold the harmonica card. Tear two gold strips and two red strips. Stick the strips and some of the border decorations from the cutting sheet on the card. Use Bradletz to hang Christmas decorations on the knots. Copy pattern K twice onto red paper and cut out the largest triangles. Stick the candles on the card using foam tape.

Card 4

Extra materials:
❏ Fiskars border ornament punch (Rope)
❏ Gold text sticker
❏ Circle cutter

Cut the card to size (14.85 x 21 cm) using harmonica ruler E. Cut, score and fold the harmonica card. Use the template to cut two semicircles. Use the circle cutter to cut out two gold circles (Ø 5 cm). Cut two 3 cm wide gold strips and one 4.5 cm wide gold strip. Punch the 3 cm strips on one side and the 4.5 cm strip on both sides. Fold the strip for the middle in two and stick one side on the card. Allow it to dry and then stick the other side on the card. Fold the card closed so that the paper sits in the fold nicely. Stick everything on the card. Stick the candles on the card using foam tape.

CHRISTMAS DECORATIONS

Flat Christmas cards

The cards measure 11 x 14.85 cm, but still fit in a standard envelope.

What you need:
- Card: dark red CA519 (P43), dark green CA309 (P18), pink C352 and orange C453

Card 1

Extra materials:
- 2 cutting sheets: Marjoleine orange Christmas decorations
- Gold line stickers
- Gold text sticker

Cut the card to size (14.85 x 21 cm) using harmonica ruler E. Use the top shape for the first set of two lines. Use the bottom shape for the third set of two lines. Note: do not score the last vertical line. Cut, score and fold the card. Slide the left-hand part of the card under the cut out shape. Decorate the card with line stickers and a text sticker. Cut out two orange rectangles (5 x 8cm) and two dark green squares (4.5 x 4.5 cm). Make the Christmas decorations 3D.

Card 2

Extra materials:
- 2 cutting sheets: Marjoleine orange Christmas decorations
- Gold star line stickers

Cut the card to size (14.85 x 21 cm) using harmonica ruler E. Use the top shape for the first set of two lines. Use the bottom shape for the third set of two lines. Note: do not score the last vertical line. Cut, score and fold the card. Slide the left-hand part of the card under the cut out shape. Use the extra cutting lines in the template to cut the half-labels. Stick the half-labels behind the cut out shapes of the card. Slide the left-hand part of the card under the cut out shape. Decorate the card with line stickers. Make the Christmas decorations 3D.

Card 3

Extra materials:
- 3 cutting sheets: Marjoleine pink Christmas decorations
- Gold star line stickers

Cut the card to size (14.85 x 21 cm) using harmonica ruler E. Use the top shape for the first set of two lines. Use the bottom shape for the third set of two lines. Note: do not score the last vertical line. Cut, score and fold the card. Use the extra cutting lines in the template to cut the half-stars. Stick the half-stars behind the cut out shapes of the card. Slide the left-hand part of the card under the cut out shape. Decorate the card with line stickers. Cut out two pink squares (5 x 5 cm) and two dark red squares (4.5 x 4.5 cm). Make the Christmas decorations 3D.

Card 4

Extra materials:
- 3 cutting sheets: Marjoleine pink Christmas decorations
- Gold line stickers
- Gold text sticker

Cut the card to size (14.85 x 21 cm) using harmonica ruler E. Use the top shape for the first set of two lines. Use the bottom shape for the third set of two lines. Note: do not score the last vertical line. Cut, score and fold the card. Slide the left-hand part of the card under the cut out shape. Copy pattern K four times onto printing paper and cut the shapes out slightly bigger. Use the Pritt roller to stick two shapes on pink card and cut the largest triangle out carefully. Use the Pritt roller to stick two shapes on dark red card and cut the smallest triangle out carefully. Decorate the card and the dark red triangles with line stickers. Make the Christmas decorations 3D.

Many thanks to:
Kars & Co. B.V. in Ochten, the Netherlands, and craft shop Crealies in Amersfoort, the Netherlands, for providing the materials.

Shopkeepers can order the materials used from Kars & Co B.V. and Papicolor (card) in the Netherlands.

The materials can be ordered from craft shop Crealies, Anna Boelensgaarde 23, 3824 BR Amersfoort, the Netherlands, +31 (0)33 4564052 (until 6 p.m.).
The shop is open on appointment.
E-mail: info@crealies.nl. Also see www.crealies.nl. If you wish to remain informed about what I have in store for you in the future, then complete the form on the website.